How Can We See A Return To The Bible?

How Can We See A Return To The Bible?

D. Martyn Lloyd-Jones

Kept Pure Press

How Can We See A Return To The Bible?

As we are met together on this great and interesting occasion, it seems to me that there are two main things which we need to do. The first is to remember and commemorate the printing of the Authorized Version of the Bible in 1611. The second great purpose of this gathering is to call back the people of this nation to the Bible.

I will take the second purpose first. Why should we come together in this manner and call the men and women of this country back to the consideration of this book which we call the Bible? There are many answers that can be given to that question, but what I regard as the most urgent reason of all is simply that the conditions in which we find ourselves at this very moment are, in the main, due to the departure of men and women from the Word of God.

This is true, in the first place, with regard to the Christian church herself. We are here, I take it, to be honest and to search ourselves. These are no days for coming together just to enjoy ourselves. The times are evil; the times are out of joint. I trust we are all here animated with a desire to do something, and to discover what we have to do, in order to deal with the appalling conditions which prevail round and about us.

I say that the condition of the church herself is due to her departure from the authority of the Bible. The Christian church in this country is in a deplorable condition. The statistics tell us that only some ten percent of the people of this country claim to be even nominally Christian; ninety percent of the population is entirely outside the church! It was not always thus.

What has been the cause of this? Why the difference in the condition of our churches today as distinct from what they were a hundred years ago? I know there are many explanations put forward.

People point to the world wars, and I do not

dispute that they did contribute to it. They also point to the wireless, the television, the motor-car, and all these other agencies that are militating against the work and the appeal of the church. I am prepared to grant to such causes a certain amount of influence, but when you come to examine this question seriously and soberly, there is only one adequate answer for the fact that the masses of the people are no longer attending places of worship: It is due to the loss of the authority of the Scriptures.

And to what is that due? Without question, it was the devastating Higher Critical movement, so called, which began in Germany around the 1830s, and which subsequently came and infected this and most other countries. This meant the substitution of the mind of men and of what is called "philosophy" for divine revelation.

It was claimed that this Book must be regarded as every other book, and examined in the same way as every other book is examined. Added to this, there was the Darwinian teaching which came in 1859 and immediately became so popular. Then psychology played its part. And in these ways men began to look at this Book, not as they had hitherto looked on it throughout the centuries as the Word of the living God, but as a human word. They began to talk more and more, not about the power of the Holy Spirit in the preacher, but of his scholarship, of his knowledge of philosophy and the sciences, and of psychology. Human reason was put upon the throne, and the very pulpits of the church herself were engaged in undermining the faith of the masses of the people in this Book as the Word of God.

It is time we face these facts. We are trying to do all we can to improve the existing condition; but, if this is the major problem, is it not obvious that nothing except a rectifying of *this* can deal with the situation that confronts us? There is no question about the reason for what has happened. Men began to talk about "the assured results" of scholarship and of criticism, and the masses of the people believed these "great experts."

Tonight, of course, we know that "the assured results" are not quite as assured, and increasingly, we find the scholars having to abandon the positions which were put with such dogmatism before the people at the end of the last century and in the first fourteen years or so of this century. Not only so, we know that liberalism, the modernism, so called, which was so popular up until 1914, has become utterly outmoded. The First World War shattered it; the confidence in man and in man's own ability ended with that war. The old liberalism which emptied our churches is as dead as the dodo and utterly discredited.

Unfortunately, that does not mean that people have returned to the Book. They seem to be prepared to do everything except come back to the Book and submit themselves to it. Some of them are cleverly trying to say that you must take the message of the Book, but not the facts. Others say that God speaks in the Book through great acts, but not in propositions and not in teaching.

In other words, they still will not submit to the authority of the Book. It is they who decide what to accept and what to reject, what to believe and what not to believe, so that though the old liberalism and modernism are utterly discredited, the position in reality is no better. I am here to assert that this is one of the main causes, if not indeed the main cause, of the decline of the Christian church.

There is one other cause of present conditions which I add with regret, and that is statements made by Christian ministers from Christian pulpits, which are nothing but blank contradictions of the basic teaching of the Bible. We hear the ridicule that is poured on the doctrine of sin, the rejection of the miracles and of the precious blood of Christ, and, to cap it all, recently, a statement to the effect that we can "expect to meet atheists in heaven."

If this is true, if we are to expect to meet atheists in heaven, if a man who does not believe in God can go to heaven, why should we ask him to believe in the Bible? Why should we have a Christian church at all? If an atheist who lives a good life is to go to heaven, there is no need for the Christian church and all the organizations, and there is absolutely no need for the Scriptures. The masses of the people are outside the Christian church because they have been given the impression that the Christian church herself no longer believes in the Book as authoritative.

I say that this is the explanation not only of the state of the church, but also of the world in general, and conditions in general in this country. Look at our industrial problems which are so acute at the moment and so dangerous. Look at our social and moral problems, to which reference has already been made. What are these due to? It seems to me that there is only one adequate answer: It is that the whole notion and concept of law and of duty, of punishment and retribution, has gone.

As men have ceased to believe in the Bible, they have ceased to believe in law, in justice, and in righteousness. So the whole notion of punishment and retribution is derided and dismissed. Indeed, I am afraid we can go a step further and say that one of the major problems in this country tonight is this: That the whole idea of responsibility is disappearing rapidly.

We are approaching a state in which a prisoner standing in the dock in a law court will be examined in terms of disease, or what they call "diminished responsibility," rather than in terms of crime. The whole notion of crime is going out. A man behaves as he does, it is argued, because of the odd combination of the ductless glands in his body, or because he was not well at a particular moment. Today it is a case of diminished responsibility; there is no such thing as a crime, there is no such thing as a criminal; it is all a problem for the doctors.

So with the disappearance of the law of God goes the disappearance of belief in any law, in the notions of punishment, correction, and discipline. Thus — and I could elaborate so easily — the state of the church and of the world in general is due to this one major cause: There is no authority, no ultimate sanction, to which men feel compelled to bow.

If that is so, the question that should be uppermost in our minds here tonight is how to get the people back to the Bible? How can we bring them back again to this Book? There are many suggestions put before us on this subject, and I want to look at one in particular.

We have been reminded tonight, and very rightly, of the part that this Book has played in the history of the life of this country. There is no question about it; the true greatness of this country was laid down and established, whatever you may think of it politically, in the Cromwellian period and by men in the House of Commons who believed this to be the Word of the living God. You do not understand the history of this country if you do not know something about the influence of this Book.

However, I do not hesitate to say tonight that it is not the appeal to history that is needed. There are people who are so ignorant that they are not interested in the past, or in the past glory of this country. They think they have got something better.

Others — and the statesmen particularly are very fond of doing this — talk about the Bible and praise it as literature. Of course, as literature, it is incomparable, but merely to tell people that this is "great literature" is not going to make them submit to its message. Look, they say, at the influence it has had upon the great masterpieces of our literature. Perfectly true, but the average man is not interested in that sort of thing; he is out for his bingo, or whatever he may chance to call his pleasure. That is not the way to bring them back.

What else can we do? Well, there are many who

are engaged in a kind of defense of the Bible. That is sometimes called apologetics. I am not here to say a word against it. Archaeology comes into that department, and we thank God for it and for Professor Wiseman as one of the distinguished people who are practicing in this realm, but that is not going to be enough either.

I agree with what Spurgeon said about this: "You don't defend a lion, you just let him loose." and the same is true of the Bible. Apologetics are all right as far as they go and they can be helpful in strengthening the faith, but we are living in a period when we need something much more. Still less must we fall back upon any tendency to accommodate the teaching of the Bible to modern learning and to modern views.

Sometimes, I fear, I see a tendency to do that, even among evangelical people. Why should we be afraid of the scientist? He has no facts which interfere with this Book. We must not accommodate them; we must not try to placate people and please them. That is not the way to handle this Book.

And now I must say a word — and I do so with considerable hesitation and trepidation — but it seems to me that, if we are to face the facts, this is unavoidable. I suppose that the most popular of all the proposals at the present time for bringing people back to Scripture is this: Let's have a new translation of the Bible.

We have had one in this year, 1961 [The New English Bible]. The argument is that the people are not reading the Bible any longer because they do not understand its language, its archaic terms. "What does your modern man, what does your modern Teddy boy know about justification, sanctification, and all these biblical terms?" That is the question.

"No," they say, "It is no good; they cannot understand the Bible," and so we are told that the one thing necessary is to have a translation which Tom, Dick, and Harry will understand. I began to feel about six months ago that we had almost reached a stage at which the Authorized Version was being dismissed, to be thrown into the limbo of things forgotten, no longer of any value.

Need I apologize for saying a word in favor of the Authorized Version in *this* gathering? Well, whatever you may think, I am going to do it, and I am going to do it without any apology.

As I read the Christian periodicals earlier this year — and I am sorry to have to add, even the evangelical ones — and all the articles about this new translation, I almost began to think for a moment that the letters NEB stood for New *Evangelical* Bible.

Everybody seemed to have succumbed to the ballyhoo, the propaganda, and the advertising. I began to wonder whether evangelical people really had lost the vital spark; but, thank God, by to-night I think I see signs of a recovery and a return to sanity.

We must examine this for a moment. Let us, first of all, be clear about the basic proposition laid down by the Protestant reformers that we must have a Bible which is, as they put it, "understanded of the people." That is common sense; that is obvious.

We all agree too that we must never be obscurantist; we must never approach the Bible in a mere antiquarian spirit. Nobody wants to be like that, nor to defend such attitudes, but there is a very grave danger incipient in much of the argument that is being presented today for these new translations. There is a danger of our surrendering something that is vital and essential.

Look at it like this. Take the argument about the terms that the modern man does not understand, the words "justification," "sanctification," and so on. I want to ask a question: When did the ordinary man ever understand those terms?

I am told the modern Teddy boy does not understand them, but consider the colliers to whom John Wesley and George Whitefield used to preach in the eighteenth century. Did they understand them? They had not even been to a day school, an elementary school. They could not read, they could not write. Yet these were the terms which they heard, and the Authorized Version was the version used. This is a very specious argument, but it does not hold water. The common people have *never* understood these terms.

However, I want to add something to this. We must be very careful in using such an argument against the Authorized Version, for the reason that the very nature and character of the truth which the Bible presents to us is such that it is extremely difficult to put into words at all.

We are not describing an animal or a machine; we are concerned here with something which is spiritual, something which does not belong to this world at all, and which, as the apostle Paul in writing to the Corinthians, reminds us, "the princes of this world" do not know.

Human wisdom is of no value here; it is a spiritual truth; it is something that is altogether different. This is truth about God primarily, and because of that, it is a mystery. There is a glory attached to it, there is a wonder, and something which is amazing. The apostle Paul, who probably understood it better than most, looking at its contents, stands back and says, "Great is the mystery of godliness" (1 Timothy 3:16).

Yet we are told, "It must be put in such simple terms and language that anybody taking it up and reading it is going to understand all about it." My friends, this is nothing but sheer nonsense! What we must do is to educate the masses of the people *up* to the Bible, not bring the Bible *down* to their level.

One of the greatest troubles in life today is that everything is being brought down to the same level; everything is being cheapened. The common man is made the standard and the authority; he decides everything, and everything has got to be brought down to him. You are getting it on your wireless, your television, in your newspapers; everywhere standards are coming down and down. Are we to do this with the Word of God? I say, No!

What has always happened in the past has been this: An ignorant, illiterate people in this country and in foreign countries, coming into salvation, have been educated *up* to the Book and have begun to understand it, and to glory in it, and to praise God for it. I am here to say that we need to do the same at this present time.

What we need, therefore, is not to replace the Authorized Version with what, I am tempted at times to call, the ITV edition of the Bible [in 1961, ITV was the only British television channel financed by advertising]. We need rather to teach and to train people up to the standard and the language and the dignity and the glory of the old Authorized Version.

I am here to suggest that we ought to protest against the dropping of great words like "propitiation" and "redemption" which are very essential to a true understanding of our gospel. And I protest against a translation that translates 2 Timothy 3:16 like this: "Every inspired scripture has its use for teaching the truth." That is an obvious statement, but it is not what the apostle Paul wrote.

The correct translation is "*All* Scripture is God-breathed and is profitable." Paul does not speak of "every Scripture that is inspired" because every Scripture *is* inspired. The translators have perpetuated the error of the Revised Version, which even the Revised Standard Version of America has corrected and brought back to the translation of the Authorized Version.

As I leave this aspect of the matter, my only remaining comment upon this new version, which is so popular, is to quote two statements, first from the *Times Literary Supplement* of March 24th.

This is not a Christian publication, but it is a very scholarly one, and a very learned one, and this is what a contributor says: "What then is lost in this new translation is dimension in depth and in time, and with dimension, beauty and mystery. In short," he goes on, "insofar as religion is rational, social, simple, communal, historical, the new Bible may help. Insofar as religion touches and satisfies men's deepest aspirations and needs, it is almost all loss."

Such is the opinion of the *Times Literary Supplement*. It is not the view of some ignorant evangelical like myself, or of Mr. Terence Brown [The General Secretary of the Trinitarian Bible Society] who has been so vilified. Here is a learned writer in the *Times Literary Supplement*.

Let me also quote to you an Archbishop of the Anglican communion, the Very Rev. Philip Harrington who is the Anglican Archbishop of Quebec, a learned, scholarly man and the author of two massive volumes on the early Christian church. This is how he writes: "The intelligent reader will find much of it that is helpful and even illuminating, but he must keep his old Authorized Version by his side in order to find out what the apostles or prophets actually said, if that is what he wants to know."

I am free to confess that I came nearer to

becoming an Anglican when I read that than ever in my life, but the Archbishop does not stop at that point — there are archbishops and *archbishops* it seems to me! — he adds: "When the old and new differ in meaning, King James, at least in the Revised Version of 1881, will be correct ninety-nine times out of a hundred." That is the opinion of the Anglican Archbishop of Quebec, writing this year on the New English Bible.

Very well, my friends, let me say a word for the old book, the old Authorized Version. It was translated by fifty-four men, every one of them a great scholar, and published in 1611. And here is another thing to commend it to you: This Authorized Version came out at a time when the church had not yet divided. I mean by that she had not yet divided into Anglican and Nonconformist. I think there is an advantage even in that. They were all still as one, with very few exceptions, when the Authorized Version was produced.

Another important point to remember is this: The Authorized Version was produced some time after that great climactic event which we call the Protestant Reformation. There had been time by then to see some of the terrible horrors of Rome and all she stood for. The early reformers had too much on their plate, as it were; Luther may have left many gaps; but when this translation was produced, there had been time for men to be able to see Rome for what she really was.

These translators were all men who were orthodox in the faith. They believed that the Bible is the infallible Word of God and they submitted to it as the final authority, as against the spurious claims of Rome, as against the appeals to the Church Fathers, and everything else. Here, I say, were fifty-four men, scholars and saintly, who were utterly submitted to the Book. You have never had that in any other version. Here and here alone you have a body of men who were absolutely committed to it, who gave themselves to it, who did not want to correct or sit in judgment upon it, whose only concern and desire was to translate it and interpret it for the masses of the people.

In view of all this, my argument is that the answer does not lie in producing new translations; they are coming out almost every week, but are they truly aiding the situation? No, and for this reason: Men no longer read the Bible *not* because they cannot understand its language, but because they do not believe in it. They do not believe in its God; they do not want it.

Their problem is not that of language and of terminology; it is the state of the heart. Therefore, what do we do about it? It seems to me there is only one thing to do, the thing that has always been done in the past: We must preach it and our preaching must be wholly based upon its authority.

We must not come to the Bible to find out whether it is true or not; we must come to find the meaning of the truth that is there. That has been the fatal error of this so-called Higher Criticism that has come to the Bible to find which part is true and which part is not. The moment you do that you are already wrong, irretrievably wrong!

We do not come to the Bible to discover whether it is true; we come to discover its meaning and its teaching, and therefore I say the only hope is that we preach its message to the people. We must preach it to them as the Word of God.

Yes, this Book is the very thing that it claims

to be. Look at its original writers! Did any one of them say it was his own idea? No, they are all unanimous in saying that it was given to them.

Some of them did not even want to write it. Isaiah, given his commission, says, "I am a man of unclean lips," I am not fit to do this. It is not a question of a great man, a great philosopher, a great thinker, who has got to tell the people what to do. No, Isaiah is given a mission and a commission. He says, I am not fit.

Jeremiah says, "I cannot speak: for I am a child." Ezekiel, when he was given his commission and message, sat stunned and amazed for seven days, and it needed the Holy Spirit to put him on his feet again. Amos said, I am a herdsman, a man tending sycamore trees. I am no prophet, nor the son of a prophet. That is what they all say. They say it is not *their* message.

Well, what is it? Oh, they say, it is "the burden of the LORD," the message of the Lord; the burden of the Lord came unto me.

Jeremiah did not want to speak, but he could not refrain; it was like a fire burning in his bones. God had given him a message and was sending him out with it. You and I must come back to this: "No prophecy of the scripture is of any private interpretation. For the prophecy came not in old time by the will of man: but holy men of God spake as they were moved by the Holy Ghost" (2 Peter 1:20-21).

That is the authority. Look what our Lord says about it. He refers to the Scriptures using phrases such as "It is written." He believed the Old Testament; he believed it all. He says, "the scripture cannot be broken" (John 10:35): who are we to dispute it? And the apostles — look at their attitude to Scripture; they constantly refer to it and quote it. For them it is the final argument; it settles all disputes.

We must present the Bible as the Word of God, not the words of men, but the Word of the living God: God speaking about himself; God speaking about men; God speaking about life; God telling us what he is going to do about a fallen world. That is what we need to preach with certainty, with assurance.

Let us tell the people about its marvel, that though it contains sixty-six books, written at different times and in different centuries, there is only one message in it. Let us tell them about fulfilled prophecy. Let us point out to them how things prophesied and predicted hundreds of years before the events were actually verified in the fullest and minutest detail.

Let us *tell* them. They do not know it. It is for us to proclaim the Word of God, and especially at this critical time in our history.

Let us tell people something about its message. It is the only book that explains life. It is the only book that explains the world as it is tonight.

We have been told now for nearly a century that the world is advancing, that man is becoming more and more perfect, that with more and more education and scientific knowledge there will be no more war.

The problem was, they said, that people did not know one another. They did not meet. If only they met, they would all love one another and embrace one another; but now that we are meeting so constantly, we cannot live together for even a few seconds! You see, there is no explanation except the explanation that is given in this Book.

"There is no peace, saith my God, to the

wicked" (Isaiah 57:21). You can be clever, you can be mighty and great and strong, you can be a great philosopher, and be very wealthy, you can own the whole world — but you will never know peace, either as an individual or among men and nations, while you are wicked. The Bible alone has the explanation. It is man's sin, man's rebellion against God.

You see, you must come back to theology; you must seek the Book and discover its message, its theology, its doctrines. If you evangelical people are against doctrine you will never get people back to the Bible.

It is not enough just to read a few verses. You must dig down and get the doctrine, the doctrine of a wholly absolute God, who is the creator of the ends of the earth, and who is the judge of the whole earth.

Man is not something that came out of some primeval slime, but a creature made in the image of God, given something of the stamp of the eternal Lord of creation, meant to live in communion and correspondence with his creator! But man has fallen into sin, has asserted his own will-power, has said that he is autonomous, that he can arrange his life, that he does not need God, he does not need God's direction and God's Word: That is why the world is in trouble.

This is what we must tell people; we must try not just to defend the Bible but to preach its truth. Tell men that they are in their present state because the world has turned its back upon God. That is why this twentieth century is so appalling. It is the century of all centuries that has asserted itself and its own will and, its own understanding over and against God and his truth and his eternal will.

We must tell them this, we must tell them very plainly and without any apology that the wrath of God has been revealed from heaven "against all ungodliness and unrighteousness of men" (Romans 1:18).

We must tell them that the very history of this century, with its two awful wars and all its present horrors, is due to the same thing. These things are a part of the judgment of God. The apostle Paul puts it thus in Romans 1, that one way in which God punishes men is, that he abandons people to themselves. He "gave them over to a reprobate mind" (vs. 28). I believe this is what is happening tonight; it is to me the only explanation of this present century.

God is saying to us, "Very well, you said you could live without me; you said you could make a perfect world without my laws, without my Word, without my truth — get on with it, see what you make of it!" And this is what we have made of it: Man a creature of lust, self-centered and selfish, fighting all others. War is inevitable while man is in that condition. The Bible alone explains this. And when you turn to the future it is exactly the same thing: There is no light for the future anywhere except in this Book.

There are people who, in the name of Christianity, are still saying that if we only preach this message we can put an end to wars. Never! The Bible asserts that there shall be wars and rumors of wars right to the end. While man is evil and sinful and the creature of lust, there will be wars.

Christianity has not come into the world to put an end to war; it has not come to reform the world. What has it come for? It has come to save us from the destruction that is coming to the world.

This Book asserts a judgment, an end of history. God in Christ will judge the whole world in righteousness, sending those who have turned their backs upon him, refused his offer of salvation in Christ, to everlasting perdition, and ushering the saints into the glory of "new heavens and a new earth, wherein dwelleth righteousness" (2 Peter 3:13).

Christian people, we must proclaim to the world that we are not afraid of the morrow. We are not afraid of what the nations may do.

We know that an evil world is under condemnation, and that the only course of safety and of wisdom is to come in penitence and contrition to the Son of God, our blessed Lord and Saviour, who came out of eternity, who died for our sins, and who will come again to receive his own unto himself. That, it seems to me, is the thing to which we are called.

We must preach the Bible's message without fear or favor and with the holy boldness of the apostles of old, not merely to say it, but to have the Holy Ghost upon us as we do so. Pray for power to proclaim it so that it shall become like "a hammer that breaketh the rock in pieces" (Jeremiah 23:29).

Or, in the words of the apostle Paul, the message must be seen to be "mighty through God to the pulling down of strong holds; casting down imaginations, and every high thing that exalteth itself against the knowledge of God, and bringing into captivity every thought to the obedience of Christ" (2 Corinthians 10:4-5). That is our calling.

> O Word of God incarnate,
> O wisdom from on high,
> O truth unchanged, unchanging,
> O light of our dark sky!
>
> O make thy Church, dear Saviour,
> A lamp of burnished gold,
> To bear before the nations,
> Thy true light as of old.

About The Author

David Martyn Lloyd-Jones (December 20, 1899 — March 1, 1981) was a Welsh Protestant minister and medical doctor who was influential in the Reformed, or Calvinistic, wing of evangelicalism in the 20th century. For nearly thirty years, he was the minister of Westminster Chapel in London.

Early Life and Ministry

Lloyd-Jones was born in Cardiff and raised in Llangeitho, Ceredigion. His father was a grocer, and he had two brothers (Harold died during the 1918 flu pandemic, while Vincent went on to become a High Court judge). Llangeitho is associated with the Welsh Methodist revival, as it was the location of Daniel Rowland's ministry.

Attending a London grammar school between

1914 and 1917, and then St. Bartholomew's Hospital as a medical student in 1921, Lloyd-Jones started work as assistant to the Royal Physician, Sir Thomas Horder. He obtained an M.D. from London University and became a member of the Royal College of Physicians.

After struggling for two years over what he sensed was a calling to preach, Lloyd-Jones returned to Wales in 1927, having married Bethan Phillips (with whom he later had two children, Elizabeth and Ann), accepting an invitation to minister at a church in Aberavon (Port Talbot).

Westminster Chapel

After a decade ministering in Aberavon, he went back to London in 1939, where he had been appointed as associate pastor of Westminster Chapel, working alongside G. Campbell Morgan.

The day before he was officially to be accepted into his new position, World War II broke out in Europe. During the same year, he became the president of the Inter-Varsity Fellowship of Students (known today as the Universities and Colleges Christian Fellowship). During the war, he and his family moved to Haslemere, Surrey. Campbell retired in 1943, leaving Lloyd-Jones as the sole Pastor of Westminster Chapel.

Lloyd-Jones was well known for his style of expository preaching and the Sunday morning and evening meetings at which he officiated drew crowds of several thousand, as did the Friday evening Bible studies, which were, in effect, sermons in the same style. He would take many months, even years, to expound a chapter of the Bible verse-by-verse.

His sermons were often fifty-minutes to an hour in length and they attracted many students from universities and colleges in London. These sermons were also transcribed and printed (virtually verbatim) in the weekly *Westminster Record*, which was read avidly by those who enjoyed his preaching.

Later Life

Lloyd-Jones retired from his ministry at Westminster Chapel in 1968, following a major operation. For the rest of his life, he concentrated on editing his sermons to be published, counseling other ministers, answering letters, and attending conferences.

Perhaps his most famous publication is a 14-volume series of commentaries on the Paul's Epistle to the Romans, the first volume of which was published in 1970.

Despite spending most of his life ministering in England, Lloyd-Jones cherished his roots in Wales. He faithfully supported the "Evangelical Movement" of Wales and was a regular speaker at their conferences, preaching in both English and Welsh.

Lloyd-Jones preached his final sermon on June 8, 1980 at Barcombe Baptist Chapel. After a lifetime of work, he died peacefully in his sleep at Ealing on March 1, 1981 (St. David's Day) and was buried at Newcastle Emlyn, near Cardigan, West Wales. A well-attended thanksgiving service was held at Westminster Chapel on April 6.

This biography was adapted from the website of the Martyn Lloyd-Jones Trust. More information about the trust can be found on the next page.

Offering some 1,600 digitally restored sermons, a new generation of Christians around the world can now benefit from Dr. Martyn Lloyd-Jones' clear teaching, brilliant insight, and unwavering commitment to the Gospel of Jesus Christ.

Lloyd-Jones has been described as "a great pillar of the 20th century Evangelical Church." Thousands flocked to hear his "full-blooded" gospel preaching, described by one hearer as "logic on fire."

Visit the MLJ Trust website at *mljtrust.org* or by using the QR code.

Kept Pure Press

Kept Pure Press is dedicated to defending the authenticity of the traditional text of Holy Scripture (Ginsburg/Bomberg Hebrew Masoretic Text and F.H.A. Scrivener's edition of the Greek New Testament) and the accuracy of our common version (The Authorized, or King James, Version).

In addition to booklets like this, free articles, videos, sermons, and lectures may be found at the online webzine: Text & Translation

Visit the webzine at *textandtranslation.org* or by using the QR code.